Writing Skills

Grade 3

Flash Kids

© 2006 by Flash Kids
Adapted from *Experiences with Writing Styles Grade 3*
© 1998 by Steck-Vaughn Company
and *Writing Skills Grade 3*
© 2003 by Steck-Vaughn Company
Licensed under special arrangement with Harcourt Achieve.

Illustrated by Rémy Simard

ISBN: 978-1-4114-0481-6

Please submit all inquiries to FlashKids@bn.com

Printed and bound in Canada
Lot #:
20 22 23 21
10/13

Flash Kids
A Division of Barnes & Noble
122 Fifth Avenue
New York, NY 10011

Dear Parent,

Reading and writing well are essential tools for success in all school subjects. In addition, many states now include writing assessments in their standardized tests. There may be no precise formula for good writing, but through studying samples and practicing different styles, your child will build the skills and versatility to approach any writing assignment with ease and confidence.

Each of the six units in this fun, colorful workbook focuses on a unique type of writing that your third-grader may be required to use in school or may wish to pursue in his or her free time. These types include personal narrative, descriptive writing, story, informative writing, opinion and comparative writing, and short report. The first half of each unit reinforces writing aspects such as putting ideas in a sequence, using descriptive details, working with a thesaurus, and using proofreading marks, in addition to providing fun, inspirational writing ideas for your child to explore alone or with a friend. The second half of each unit focuses on a practice paper that exemplifies the writing type. After your child reads the practice paper, he or she will analyze it, prepare a writing plan for his or her own paper, write a first draft, revise it, and, lastly, allow you or a friend to score it.

Here are some helpful suggestions for getting the most out of this workbook:

- Provide a quiet place to work.
- Go over the directions together.
- Encourage your child to do his or her best.
- Check each activity when it is complete.
- Review your child's work together, noting good work as well as points for improvement.

As your child completes the units, help him or her maintain a positive attitude about writing. Provide writing opportunities such as a journal, in which your child can write about things that happen each day and can keep a running list of topics or story ideas for future writing projects. Read your child's stories aloud at bedtime, and display his or her writing in your home.

Most importantly, enjoy this time you spend together. Your child's writing skills will improve even more with your dedication and support!

Proofreading Marks

Use the following symbols to help make proofreading faster.

MARK	MEANING	EXAMPLE
◯	spell correctly	*like* I ⟨liek⟩ dogs.
⊙	add period	They are my favorite kind of pet⊙
⋏	add comma	I also like cats⋏ birds, and bunnies.
?	add question mark	What kind of pet do you have?
≡	capitalize	My dog's name is scooter. ≡
/	make lowercase	He has /Brown spots.
ℓ	take out	He likes to t̶o̶ run and play.
⋏	add	He even likes to get ⋏ bath. *a*
∿	switch	Afterward he ⟨all⟩shakes⟩ over.
¶	indent paragraph	¶ I love my dog, Scooter. He is the best pet I have ever had. Every morning he wakes me with a bark. Every night he sleeps with me.
⌄ ⌄	add quotation marks	⌄You are my best friend,⌄ I tell him.

Table of Contents

uNIT 1: Personal Narrative

HOW MUCH DO YOU KNOW?

Read the three sentences. They are out of order. Label each one *beginning*, *middle*, or *ending*.

1. A patch of lettuce grew under my window.

   _____

2. I planted seeds under my window.

   _____

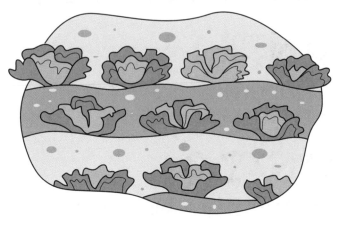

3. Mom picked the lettuce for a salad.

   _____

Choose the title you think is more interesting. Draw a line under it. Write a sentence to tell why you think so.

4. A Black Dog   The Tallest Dog in the World

   _____

Write a story about how you got to school today.

_____

_____

_____

_____

Analyzing a Personal Narrative

> **A PERSONAL NARRATIVE**
> - has one topic
> - tells about the writer
> - has sentences that tell what happens in the beginning, the middle, and the ending
> - uses the words *I*, *me*, and *my*

Read each group of three sentences. They are out of order.
Label each one *beginning*, *middle*, or *ending*.

1. a. I put my palm tree near a window.

    _____

    b. I bought a potted palm tree at the plant store.

    _____

    c. I brought the palm tree home.

    _____

2. a. After reading that, I took my palm tree into the shower with me.

    _____

    b. The book said that palm trees should be washed often.

    _____

    c. I read about palm trees in a book about plants.

    _____

Connecting Ideas in a Sequence

To write a personal narrative, good writers tell about things in the order in which they happen.

Read each paragraph. Then number the events below it in the order in which they happened.

1.   We looked at the four eggs on the leaves of the tomato plant. Each egg was about as big as the head of a pin. During the week, we watched as the pale green eggs changed to yellowish-green and then almost white. One morning something inside started to cut a hole in one of the eggs. Soon, a tiny caterpillar crawled out of the egg. Within a short time, all the eggs had hatched.

_____ The eggs changed to yellowish-green, then white.

_____ The eggs hatched.

_____ We saw pale green eggs on the tomato leaves.

2.   The first thing the pale caterpillars did was start to eat tomato leaves. We watched as they grew and grew. After a few days, the skin of each one split down the back. Each caterpillar crawled out of the old skin. There was a new, bigger skin underneath. Each caterpillar was about four inches long and bright green in color.

_____ The caterpillars began to eat the tomato leaves.

_____ The caterpillars were four inches long and bright green.

_____ The skin of the caterpillars split for the first time.

Capturing the Reader's Interest

> Good writers capture the reader's interest by creating
> - a catchy title
> - a strong beginning sentence

Choose the title you think is more interesting. Circle it. Write a sentence to tell why you think so.

1. Mysteries, Monsters, and Untold Secrets   Things We Don't Understand

   _____

2. Jim Saves Time   A Wrinkle in Time

   _____

3. The No-Return Trail   The Country Road

   _____

4. From the Mixed-Up Files of Mrs. Basil E. Frankenweiler   The Day I Ran Away from Home

   _____

5. Willie Bea's Day   Willie Bea and the Day the Martians Landed

   _____

Using the Thesaurus

- A *thesaurus* is a book of *synonyms*, or words that have nearly the same meaning.

- *Antonyms*, or words that mean the opposite of the entry word, follow the synonyms.

Replace the underlined word with a synonym or an antonym. Use a thesaurus or a dictionary to find synonyms and antonyms. Write the new word on the line.

1. Dan will <u>get</u> a baby duck in the spring.

   synonym: _____

2. Dan is very <u>lucky</u>.

   synonym: _____

3. A baby deer would make a <u>good</u> pet.

   antonym: _____

4. Pets <u>need</u> special food and water.

   synonym: _____

5. It is best not to <u>purchase</u> a pet you can't keep.

   synonym: _____

6. Baby raccoons are the <u>most</u> popular wild animal pets.

   antonym: _____

7. It is very <u>kind</u> to keep a raccoon in a cage.

   antonym: _____

Proofreading a Personal Narrative

Proofread the beginning of the personal narrative, paying special attention to end marks. Use the Proofreading Marks to correct at least seven errors.

PROOFREADING MARKS

⬭	spell correctly
⊙	make lowercase
⌃·	add period
?	add comma
=	add question mark
/	capitalize
ℒ	take out
∧	add
∿	switch
¶	indent paragraph
⌄ ⌄	add quotation marks

See the chart on Page 4 to learn how to use these marks

Uncle John has always been my favorite uncle What a surprise we all had last summer Late one evening there was a knock at the back door. Can you guess who was standing on our back steps Of course, it was Uncle John He had a backpack, a small suitcase, and an armload of gifts.

Uncle John's present for me was a bright blew T-shirt. it has a picture of an old castle on the back. Uncle John bought the shirt for me when he was traveling in England last year I wore that shirt every day wile Uncle John was staying with us

Uncle John has been to many different parts of the world, and he loved telling us about his adventures. Listening to his stories was almost as much fun as going along on Uncle John's trips

Order a Story

Write one or two sentences of a story in each of the boxes on this page. The boxes should be out of order. Ask a friend to try to put the boxes in order. He or she should read the story aloud to see if it makes sense.

Write Your Own Sentences

Pick your favorite kind of dinosaur. Draw a picture of that dinosaur. Under the picture, write three sentences that tell about it.

Write about Wishes

Talk with a friend about wishes. Make a list of your wishes.

_____   _____

_____   _____

_____   _____

Write four sentences about your wishes. Be sure to revise and proofread your sentences.

_____

_____

_____

_____

_____

_____

A Practice Personal Narrative

SAVE JACK

I remember when I met Danny. He came at just the right time. I was new in town, and I needed a friend. I didn't know that Danny would become my best friend.

The summer I was eight years old, my family moved. We didn't move to a new house down the street. We moved to a new town 500 miles away. I hated leaving my friends. I was so sad when we left.

Here I was in a new town and had no friends. I wouldn't let myself think of the day school would start.

There were lots of people in my class, but I felt lonely. I didn't see any friends. I only saw kids I had never seen before. They all seemed to know and like each other. I wanted someone to notice me, and they did.

One boy called me "Four Eyes" because I wore glasses. "That's an old joke," I thought, but it still bothered me. A second boy called me "Scaredy Cat." I'm not sure why. I guess I looked scared. This wasn't the kind of attention I wanted.

At recess, everyone played ball and ran races. I stood against the building. I saw all of them, but they didn't see me. If I had been younger, I probably would have cried.

When I went home that afternoon, I went straight to my room. I didn't have any homework. I just didn't want Mom to see how unhappy I was.

On Tuesday, I met Danny. "Would you like to play ball at recess?" he asked. At first, I was too surprised to answer. It took a minute to find the word I needed. "Yes," I said gladly. I was happy to play ball with Danny. Suddenly, school was starting to get better. That feeling lasted until I walked home that afternoon.

After school, another boy from my class started to walk home with me. I was still thinking about Danny. Tom wasn't anything like Danny. In fact, he wasn't friendly at all. He started teasing me about being new. "Look at the new kid. Where did you come from? You look green to me." He said more, but I stopped paying attention. A couple of blocks later, Tom got tired and left me alone. By that time, I had almost forgotten how much I liked Danny. All I could think about was how many kids acted like Tom.

When I got to school on Wednesday, Danny was the first person I saw. I couldn't believe it. He was talking to Tom. I decided to go up to them. When I came near, Danny stopped talking. I didn't know what that meant until recess.

At recess, Danny and I were playing soccer. Tom came over and asked if he could play, too. Danny said, "Sure." I didn't know what to say.

On Thursday, more kids came over to play. We had enough people to make two teams. Recess was getting better.

That afternoon, Danny walked home with me even though he lived on a different street. I wondered if he was trying to stop other kids from bothering me. It didn't really matter. I liked

Danny, and he seemed to like me.

On Friday, I learned something about Danny. He was talking to some kids in my class. As I walked up, I heard him say, "Some of us have started a special club called the Save Jack Club. Would you like to join?"

I couldn't believe my ears. Danny had started a club just for me. He had made all the kids in my class part of the club. The kids liked Danny a lot. When they saw that he was my friend, they wanted to be my friends, too. Danny rescued me. I was more than just the new kid now. Danny was my new best friend. He still is.

Respond to the Practice Paper

Write your answers to the following questions or directions.

1. Why did the writer write this story?

   _____

   _____

2. How did the writer feel in the beginning of the story? How do you know?

   _____

   _____

3. How did the writer feel at the end of the story? How do you know?

   _____

   _____

   _____

4. Write a paragraph to summarize this story. Use these questions to help you write your summary:
   • What is the story about?
   • What happens first? Second? Third?
   • How does the story end?

   _____

   _____

   _____

   _____

   _____

   _____

Analyze the Practice Paper

Read "Save Jack" again. As you read, think about how the writer wrote the story. Write your answers to the following questions.

1. How do you know that this is a personal narrative?

   _____

   _____

2. What is Jack's problem?

   _____

   _____

   _____

3. How is the problem solved?

   _____

   _____

   _____

   _____

4. How are the first paragraph and the last paragraph alike?

   _____

   _____

   _____

   _____

   _____

   _____

   _____

   _____

Writing Assignment

Think about the best friend in your life now. Think about writing a personal narrative that tells about your best friend. Use examples and details to show why this person is your best friend. Use this writing plan to help you write a first draft on the next page.

Name your friend:

▼

Tell how you and this person became friends.

▼

Give examples to show why this person is your <u>best</u> friend.

First Draft

TIPS FOR WRITING A PERSONAL NARRATIVE:

- Write from your point of view. Use the words *I* and *my* to show your readers that this is your story.

- Think about what you want to tell your reader.

- Organize your ideas into a beginning, middle, and end.

- Write an introduction that "grabs" your reader's attention.

- Write an ending for your story. Write it from your point of view.

Use your writing plan as a guide for writing your first draft of a personal narrative. Include a catchy title.

_____

_____

_____

_____

_____

_____

_____

_____

_____

(Continue on your own paper.)

Revise the Draft

Use the chart below to help you revise your draft. Check YES or NO to answer each question in the chart. If you answer NO, make notes to remind yourself how you can revise, or change, your writing to improve it.

Question	YES ✔	NO ✔	If the answer is NO, what will you do to improve your writing?
Does your story describe your best friend?			
Does your story have a strong beginning?			
Do you describe events in the order they happened?			
Does your story have an ending?			
Do you give examples to show why this person is your best friend?			
Do you tell your story from your point of view?			
Have you corrected mistakes in spelling, grammar, and punctuation?			

Use the notes in your chart and your writing plan to revise your draft.

Writing Report Card

Read your revised draft again or ask someone else to read it. Have the person who reads your paper complete the following Report Card. Revise your paper until you have no less than a Very Good Score for each item.

Title of paper: _____

Purpose of paper: ____*This is a personal narrative. It tells about my*____

____*best friend.*____

Person who scores the paper: _____

Score	Writing Goals
	Does this story have a strong beginning?
	Are the story's main ideas organized into paragraphs?
	Are there details to support each main idea?
	Are the paragraphs organized in a way that makes sense?
	Are there different kinds of sentences that help make the story interesting?
	Is there a strong ending?
	Are the story's grammar, spelling, and punctuation correct?

☺ Excellent Score   ☆ Very Good Score   + Good Score

✔ Acceptable Score   – Needs Improvement

UNIT 2: Informative Writing

HOW MUCH DO YOU KNOW?

Read the paragraph. Draw a line under the sentence that tells the main idea. Then list two details.

Animal tracks can tell you many things. For example, most cat tracks are smaller than dog tracks. Also, cat tracks are more rounded than dog tracks are. Cats usually keep their nails pulled in, but dogs can't do that. So dog tracks show nail marks.

1. _____

2. _____

Read each paragraph. Answer the questions.

A.   People who live in cities enjoy parks. Many families spend the day in the park. They do many fun things. Sometimes they bring picnic lunches.

B.   People who live in cities enjoy parks. Many families spend the entire day in the park. Sometimes my family begins the morning with a canoe ride on the deep, blue lake. Ducks and turtles watch the canoes go by. At noon, we stop for a picnic of chicken, fruit, and cake. My family spends the afternoon looking for bears, elephants, and dragons in the clouds.

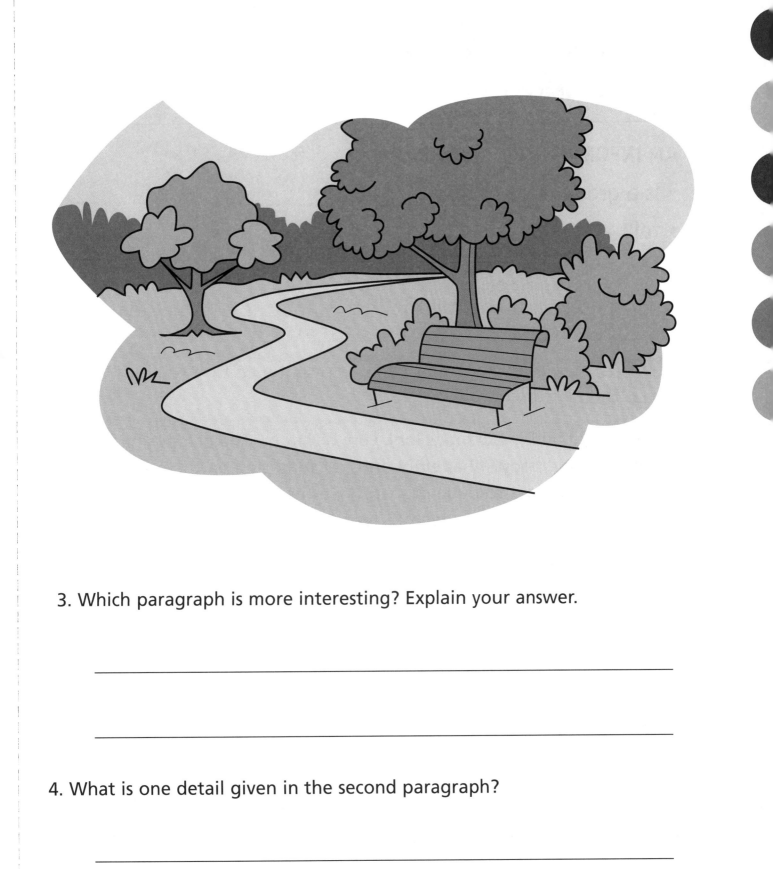

3. Which paragraph is more interesting? Explain your answer.

_____

_____

4. What is one detail given in the second paragraph?

_____

Analyzing an Information Paragraph

AN INFORMATION PARAGRAPH

- is a group of sentences
- tells about one main idea
- has a topic sentence that tells the main idea
- has detail sentences that tell facts about the main idea

Read each paragraph. Draw a line under the sentence that tells the main idea. Then list two details.

1.   The squid and the octopus look very different. The octopus has a round head and body. It has eight arms, or tentacles, on the bottom of its body. The squid is torpedo-shaped. All of its tentacles are at one end. Eight of them are the same length. Two are longer, for a total of ten.

a. _____

b. _____

2.   The squid and the octopus behave very differently. The squid can shoot through the water at great speed. The octopus moves more slowly and spends most of its time on the sea bottom.

a. _____

_____

b. _____

_____

Connecting Main Idea and Details

> **TO WRITE AN INFORMATION PARAGRAPH, GOOD WRITERS**
> - think about one main idea
> - plan interesting details to tell about the main idea

Read each group of sentences. Write *main idea* or *detail* to tell what each would be in a paragraph.

1. a. If you break off the end, you can make an herb pot.

    _____

    b. You can arrange cracked pieces into a design.

    _____

    c. A person can do a lot of things with an eggshell.

    _____

    d. You can decorate it for certain holidays.

    _____

2. a. Place the egg over a bowl.

    _____

    b. With a safety pin, make a small hole in each end of a raw egg.

    _____

    c. Slowly run water through the hollow egg to clean it out.

    _____

    d. It is easy to hollow out an egg.

    _____

Using Enough Details

GOOD WRITERS GIVE READERS

- interesting details
- clear examples

Read each paragraph. Answer the questions.

A.   Owls are best known for their ability to see at night. They can see 100 times better than humans can. Their eyes are big and do not move very easily. This is why owls' necks have to turn so far.

B.   Though they can also see well in the daytime, owls are known for seeing at night. They can see 100 times better at night than humans can, but they are color-blind. Owls' eyes are very large, and they control the light coming in by changing the size of the pupil of the eyes. Each pupil acts alone. If you stood in the sun and your friend stood in the shade, an owl could see each of you well.

1. Which paragraph is more interesting? Explain your answer.

    _____

    _____

2. What is one detail given in the second paragraph?

    _____

3. Write one example found in the second paragraph.

    _____

Keeping to the Topic

- A good writer plans a paragraph so that it shares details about one main idea.
- All the sentences in a paragraph must keep to the topic.

Read the topic sentence below. Choose the sentences that keep to the topic. Write a paragraph, using the topic sentence and the sentences you chose.

<u>A sighted person can only imagine what it is like to be blind</u>.

Put a scarf over your eyes to block out light.

Try to figure out what different foods are.

Being deaf is not easy either.

Pretend to pay for something with coins.

Try to walk into another room and sit at a table.

A person who cannot hear has different problems.

Blind people can do all these things and more.

_____

_____

_____

_____

_____

_____

_____

_____

Proofreading Information Paragraphs

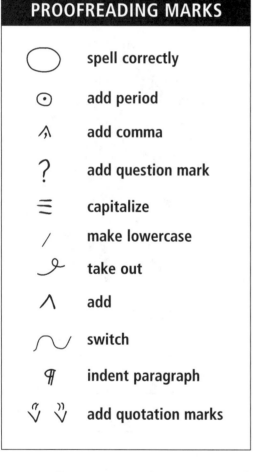

PROOFREADING MARKS

◯	spell correctly
⊙	add period
⋏	add comma
?	add question mark
≡	capitalize
/	make lowercase
ℐ	take out
∧	add
∿	switch
¶	indent paragraph
⋎ ⋎	add quotation marks

Proofread the information paragraphs, paying special attention to missing words. Use the Proofreading Marks to correct at least six errors.

Pond snails are useful in fish tanks. Pond snails will any extra food your fish leave. They will also eat some the moss that appears on the plants. The snails will eat some of moss on the glass walls of the tank, too If you have sevrel pond snails in fish tank, you will not have to clean the tank as often.

If your pond snails are having babies, be sure to remove the snails the tank. Fish will eat snail eggs. In the same way, if your fish are having babies, be sure remove the snails. Snails will eat fish eggs.

There are many different kinds snails. Their different kinds shells can add grately to the beauty of your fish tank. Not only are snails useful in keeping a tank clean, they also add interest to the tank.

Write about Zoo Animals

Choose one animal you would like to see at the zoo. Draw a picture of the animal. Then write four sentences about the animal. You might write about the animal's looks, food, and special needs.

Make a List and Write a Paragraph

With a friend, make a list of ten interesting topics to write about. Then work alone to pick one of the topics for your paragraph. Write the paragraph. Add one sentence that does not keep to your topic. Ask your friend to read your paragraph and draw a line through the sentence that does not belong.

1. _____

2. _____

3. _____

4. _____

5. _____

6. _____

7. _____

8. _____

9. _____

10. _____

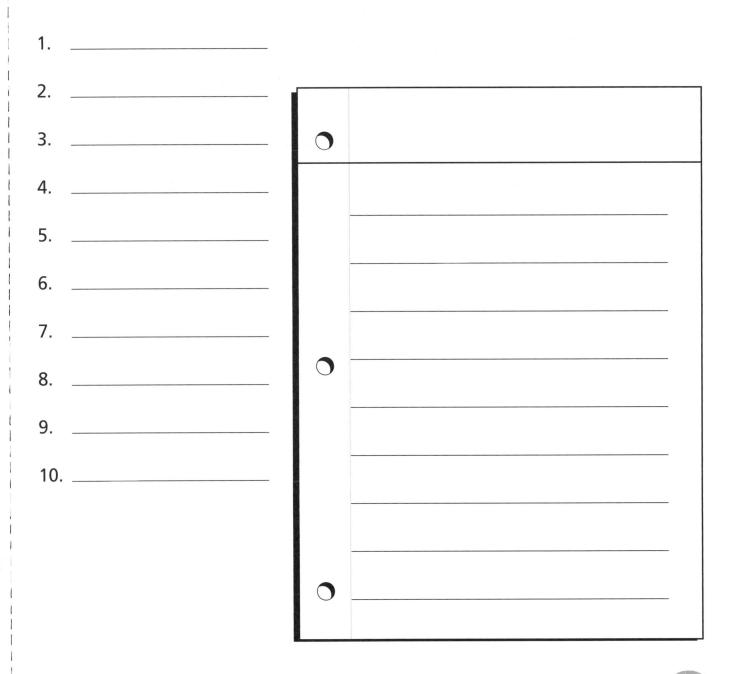

Write about Farm Animals

Write a paragraph about your favorite farm animals. Tell what those animals eat and do. Proofread and revise your paragraph.

_____

_____

_____

_____

_____

_____

_____

_____

_____

A Practice How-to Paper

MAKE A DRUM

You and your friends can each make a drum and drumsticks. Your drum can be simple or fancy. It's up to you.

The most important thing you need to make a drum is a box with a lid. The box should be round and made from cardboard. An empty oatmeal box works well. The box will vibrate, or shake, like a drum.

You will also need these things:
- Two new, unsharpened pencils
- Aluminum foil
- Tempera paint and a small paintbrush
- Colored construction paper
- Glitter, or other shiny things
- Glue
- Heavy cord or string
- Art apron or old shirt
- Old newspapers

Make the drumsticks first. Wrap each pencil in foil. Put the drumsticks away until you have finished making your drum.

Put on your apron. Spread old newspaper on your worktable. Now you are ready to decorate your drum.

First, paint the outside of the box but not the lid. Let the box dry.

Next, cut out a round piece of colored paper to cover the box lid. Glue the paper to the lid. Cut out extra pieces of colored paper to decorate the sides. Glue the pieces to the sides of the drum. You may want to glue glitter or other shiny objects on your drum, too.

Now you need to make a cord for your drum. The cord lets you hang the drum around your neck while you use your drumsticks. Hold one end of the cord at your waist. Pull the other end around your neck. Let it fall to your waist again. Cut the cord.

Ask an adult to help you punch one hole on each side of your box. The holes should be about one inch below the lid. Thread the cord through one hole. Tie two knots in the cord outside the hole. Thread the other end of the cord through the second hole. Tie two knots in the cord.

Hang the drum around your neck. Use your drumsticks to practice drumming.

Together with your friends, plan a parade. Practice tapping a beat for everyone to follow. Beat out a march or a skip. Beat out a run or a walk.

Invite your family to join you. Help them make drums, too. Together, your friends and family can make a neighborhood band.

Respond to the Practice Paper

Write your answers to the following questions or directions.

1. What does this how-to paper teach you to do?

   _____

2. What materials do you need?

   _____

   _____

   _____

   _____

3. What is the most important thing you need?

   _____

4. Why do you need a cord or a string?

   _____

   _____

5. Write a paragraph to describe a drum you would like to make. On a
   separate piece of paper, draw a picture to go with your paragraph.

   _____

   _____

   _____

   _____

Analyze the Practice Paper

Read "Make a Drum" again. As you read, think about how the writer wrote this paper. What did the writer do to help explain how to make a drum? Write your answers to the following questions or directions.

1. Why is this a good example of a how-to paper?

    _____

    _____

2. What is the first thing the writer tells you to do before you begin to make a drum?

    _____

    _____

3. Why does the writer list the materials you need to make a drum?

    _____

    _____

4. Why does the writer use words like *now*, *first*, and *next*?

    _____

    _____

5. Draw a picture to show one of the steps in making a drum.

Writing Assignment

Think about something you want to tell others how to do. Use this writing plan to help you write a first draft on the next page.

Tell what you want to tell others how to do.

List the materials you will need.

Write the steps someone should follow in order. Number the steps.

Write some sequence words that help the reader know what to do.

First Draft

TIPS FOR WRITING A HOW-TO PAPER:

- Choose one thing to teach someone.
- Think of all the materials you will need.
- Think of all the steps someone will follow.
- Use sequence words.

Use your writing plan as a guide for writing your first draft of a how-to paper. Include a catchy title.

_____

_____

_____

_____

_____

_____

_____

_____

_____

_____

_____

_____

(Continue on your own paper.)

Revise the Draft

Use the chart below to help you revise your draft. Check YES or NO to answer each question in the chart. If you answer NO, make notes to remind yourself how you can revise, or change, your writing to improve it.

Question	YES ✔	NO ✔	If the answer is NO, what will you do to improve your writing?
Does your paper teach how to do something?			
Do you include the materials someone needs?			
Do you tell the steps someone must follow?			
Are the steps in order?			
Do you use sequence words?			
Have you corrected mistakes in spelling, grammar, and punctuation?			

Use the notes in your chart and your writing plan to revise your draft.

Writing Report Card

Read your revised draft again or ask someone else to read it. Have the person who reads your paper complete the following Report Card. Revise your paper until you have no less than a Very Good Score for each item.

Title of paper: _____

Purpose of paper: ___*This is a how-to paper. It explains how to*___

___*do something.*___

Person who scores the paper: _____

Score	Writing Goals
	Does the paper teach how to do something?
	Does the paper tell the materials someone needs?
	Does the paper tell the steps someone will follow?
	Are the steps in order?
	Are there sequence words to help the reader understand?
	Are the story's grammar, spelling, and punctuation correct?

☺ Excellent Score   ☆ Very Good Score   + Good Score
✔ Acceptable Score   − Needs Improvement

UNIT 3: Descriptive Writing

HOW MUCH DO YOU KNOW?

Read the paragraphs. Underline or write the correct answer to each question below them.

Lori picked up Casey's right leg and put it into the green pants. Casey squirmed and his leg came out of the pants.

"Do you not like those green pants?" Lori asked. She picked up the red and white striped pants. Casey lay still while Lori put the pants on him.

Then Lori picked up the blue hat with a red ball on top. She tied the hat under Casey's chin. Casey shook his head. Lori pulled Casey's tail out of the hole she'd cut in the pants.

"You look cute, Casey!" Lori said.

Casey said, "Meow."

1. What color pants would Casey not wear?
   a. green
   b. red and white striped
   c. blue

2. How did Lori make the pants fit Casey?
   a. She picked the pair that fit the best.
   b. She picked the pair Casey liked the best.
   c. She cut a hole for Casey's tail.

3. What two details tell you Casey is a cat?

   _____

   _____

   _____

Analyzing a Descriptive Paragraph

> **A DESCRIPTIVE PARAGRAPH**
> • **tells what someone or something is like**
> • **paints a clear and vivid word picture**

A. Read each sentence. Write the words that describe colors, shapes, and sizes.

1. Juanita bought a thick red blanket. _____

_____

2. She carried it home in a round basket. _____

3. Her green basket had an orange pattern on it.

_____

4. As she got close to her two-story house, her tiny puppy greeted her.

5. "Hi, Zorba, you huge hound!" Juanita said. _____

6. Juanita spoiled her little brown dog. _____

7. The colorful blanket was for Zorba. _____

B. Read each sentence. Write the words that describe sounds, tastes, smells, and feelings.

8. A loud banging sound came from the kitchen.

_____

9. "What a terrific smell!" Juanita thought. _____

10. "Dad is baking another delicious pie," she said. _____

11. "It must be a sweet, moist pie," she said. _____

Observing Details

To write a descriptive paragraph, good writers pay close attention to what they will describe.

Read each paragraph. Underline the correct ending for each numbered sentence or question.

The cactus wren is the largest member of the wren family. Its back is brown with black bars and white streaks. There is a white stripe over each eye. The bird's breast is white, spotted with black.

1. The details in this paragraph tell

   a. about the bird's nest.

   b. about the bird's coloring.

   c. about the bird's life.

2. The colors of the cactus wren are

   a. black and white.

   b. brown and white.

   c. black, brown, and white.

The California poppy is sometimes called the golden poppy. It is a bright yellow color, shading to gold at its center. The flower is two or three inches across. The plant grows two feet tall. In the spring, countless millions of these plants cover California's mountainsides with gold.

3. The details in this paragraph tell

   a. about the poppy's color and size.

   b. about California's ocean.

   c. about California's weather.

4. What name does this plant not have?

   a. golden poppy

   b. mountainside poppy

   c. California poppy

Using Sensory Words and Vivid Language

> **GOOD WRITERS**
> - use sensory words to tell how someone or something looks, feels, sounds, smells, or tastes
> - use exact verbs to tell how someone or something moves

Read each sentence. Decide which one of the senses is being used. Write *look*, *feel*, *sound*, *taste*, or *smell* on the line.

1. The chimneys were outlined against a pale pink sky.

   _____

2. The morning air was very chilly. _____

3. Suddenly, a loud cry broke the silence. _____

4. A young boy poked his head out of one chimney.

   _____

5. The boy called "All up!" in a loud voice.

   _____

6. He waved his cleaning tools.

   _____

7. Then he slid into the chimney to clean it. _____

8. Later, he had some spicy cider to drink. _____

9. He warmed his hands on the hot cup. _____

10. The smell of roast pork filled the air. _____

Combining Sentences

- Good writers often combine short sentences to make writing interesting.

- Two sentences might have the same predicate. The sentences can be combined by joining the subjects with the word *and*.

Combine each pair of sentences into one sentence. Remember to join subjects with the word *and*. Write the new sentence.

1. Guppies are pets for fish tanks. Goldfish are pets for fish tanks.

   _____

   _____

2. Catfish clean harmful moss from the tank. Snails clean harmful moss from the tank.

   _____

   _____

3. Black mollies are lovely fish. Goldfish are lovely fish.

   _____

   _____

4. Guppies have live babies. Black mollies have live babies.

   _____

   _____

5. Zebra fish lay eggs. Angelfish lay eggs.

   _____

Observing Details

PROOFREADING HINT

To be a good proofreader, look for one type of error at a time.
For example, proofread once for capitalization errors,
once for punctuation errors, and once for spelling errors.

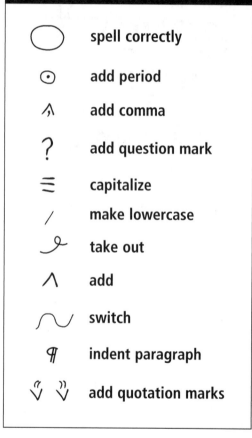

PROOFREADING MARKS	
◯	spell correctly
⊙	add period
⋏	add comma
?	add question mark
⹀	capitalize
/	make lowercase
℘	take out
⋀	add
∿	switch
¶	indent paragraph
ⱽ ⱽ	add quotation marks

Proofread the descriptive paragraphs, paying special attention to the verbs that go with sentence subjects. Use the Proofreading Marks to correct at least seven errors.

Have you ever heard of a person who likes washing dishes? My friend Dan really enjoy it. In fact, Dan washes dishes whenever he can. Dan pull a chair over to the sink so he can reach everything easily. Dan likes the lemony smell of the liquid detergent He squeezes the bottle gently and watches the liquid soap stream into the water. The soap mix with the hot water. Together, they create a mass of frothy white bubbles. When the bubbles almost reach the top of the sink, Dan turns the water off. then he carefully puts the glasses into the water.

Most of all, Dan like using a brand-new dishcloth. The cloth feel soft in Dan's hands. It has a clean smell, too. Dan rub each glass carefully with the soft, new cloth. Then he rinses the glass and sets it on the drainer.

Write about a Holiday

Choose one special holiday. Draw a picture of the holiday celebration. Write at least four sentences about it. Tell why you like the holiday and what you enjoy doing on the holiday.

Write about the Weather

Choose your favorite kind of weather. Draw a picture showing that weather. Then write four sentences to describe your picture.

Write about Food

Look through old magazines or newspapers and cut out pictures of food. Paste each picture on this page. Write sentences to describe each food.

Describe a Friend

Work with a friend. Look closely at your friend, observing at least five attractive details about him or her. Write five details that your friend would be happy to hear. Draw a picture of your friend.

_____

_____

_____

_____

_____

_____

_____

_____

_____

_____

MY FRIEND

Write about a Pet

Draw a picture of a pet. Write three sentences describing the pet.

_____

_____

_____

_____

_____

_____

A Practice Descriptive Story

MAYBE NEXT YEAR

I sat on the grass behind the field. My parents sat behind me. I watched the batter swing at the ball. "Strike one!" yelled the umpire, raising her right hand. The player got ready to hit again.

The day was hot, and the grass made my skin itch. I didn't care. This was my first live ball game. Matt, a friend from school, was the first pitcher for the White Caps that night. Our team was playing the Green Caps of Pittsfield.

We were playing at home, so the White Caps were on the field. The Green Caps were up at bat. Matt threw the second pitch. "Strike two!" cried the umpire. Matt waited until the player was ready. Then he threw again. The bat whooshed through the air, but I didn't hear it hit the ball. "Strike three!" called the umpire. Matt struck out the Green Cap.

Next, a tall boy put a green batting helmet on his head. He smacked the first ball that Matt pitched. The ball flew toward the third-base line. The Green Cap ran faster than a squirrel to first base. The ball stayed inside the line. The player was safe.

"That was some hit!" roared my father, clapping hard.

"Why are you clapping for him? He's a Green Cap," I said.

"I'm being fair, Jess. I clap for people who do a good job," Dad said. "It doesn't matter what color cap they wear."

The inning went by fast. The Green Caps had two runs. "Wow!" I said to my parents. "They're good. Will we beat them?"

"Never can tell," Mom said.

Two minutes into the second inning, the pitcher struck out our first player. Then came player number two. Player three struck out, too. The Green Caps and their families jumped up and down. They screamed wildly. Their clapping sounded like thunder. My family clapped, too.

The excitement never let up. The air was filled with claps, yells, and moans. Bats cracked, and players ran like swift cats. Their shoes kicked up clouds of dust that moved like storms across the field. Players delivered some hard hits. Umpires called some close strikes. When our team tied the score, the home crowd went wild.

Finally, it was the last inning. A Green Cap hit the ball. I could hear the coach yell, "Run, Jason, run!" Jason flew. No White Cap could keep up. He made it to first base safely. But then, he decided to steal a base. He waited until the pitcher pitched the next ball. Then he ran as fast as his legs could move. Our catcher saw the move. He threw the ball to second base. Jason was caught between first and second base. The player at second base tagged him out. The crowd roared.

That was the end of the last inning for the Green Caps. The score was 2 to 2. Now it was our team's turn. Wham! Tony smacked a long drive to center field. Then Maria hit the ball softly so it wouldn't go far. That helped the player on first base move to second. Paul popped the ball straight up. It went so high that it looked like a small, white bird.

Nancy was our next batter. She clutched the bat like a major-league player. The first two pitches were balls. Then Nancy's bat met the third pitch. The game was won.

What a game! The Green Caps and the White Caps shook hands. They told each other they had done a good job. Families hugged their kids and told them what a great game it had been. My parents and I clapped for everyone. Maybe next year I can be a White Cap.

Respond to the Practice Paper

Write your answers to the following questions or directions.

1. What was Matt's job on the team?

   _____

   _____

2. Why did Jess's father clap for the Green Caps?

   _____

   _____

3. How do you know that Jess really liked the game?

   _____

   _____

4. Write a paragraph to summarize this story. Use these questions to help
   you write your summary:
   - What is the story about?
   - What happens first? Second?
   - How does the story end?

   _____

   _____

   _____

   _____

   _____

   _____

   _____

Analyze the Practice Paper

Read "Maybe Next Year" again. As you read, think about how the writer wrote this story. Write your answers to the following questions.

1. What makes this story descriptive?

_____

_____

_____

2. What are some exciting action words the writer uses?

_____

_____

_____

3. What are some descriptions the writer uses to help you imagine what is happening in the story?

_____

_____

_____

4. The writer says that the players ran like swift cats. What is another way the writer could describe players who run fast?

_____

_____

_____

Writing Assignment

To describe something, a writer tells what he or she sees, hears, feels, tastes, and smells. The writer uses interesting words. The writer also compares things to other things, like a fast runner to a swift cat. Think about something that happened to you that you would like to describe. Use this writing plan to help you write a first draft on the next page.

What experience would you like to describe? Write it in the circle. Then write words that describe the experience on the lines.

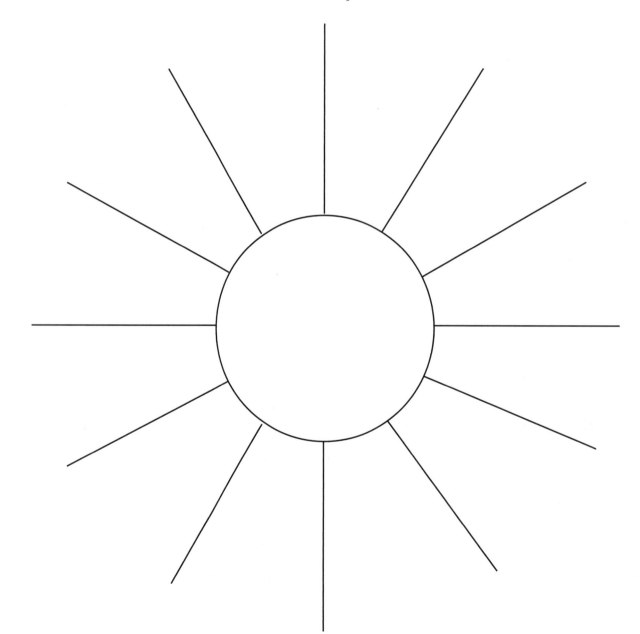

First Draft

TIPS FOR WRITING A DESCRIPTIVE STORY:

- Help readers see, smell, taste, feel, and hear what you are writing about.
- Use interesting words to help you describe.

Use your writing plan as a guide for writing your first draft of a descriptive story. Include a catchy title.

_____

_____

_____

_____

_____

_____

_____

_____

_____

_____

_____

_____

_____

(Continue on your own paper.)

Revise the Draft

Use the chart below to help you revise your draft. Check YES or NO to answer each question in the chart. If you answer NO, make notes to remind yourself how you can revise, or change, your writing to improve it.

Question	YES ✔	NO ✔	If the answer is NO, what will you do to improve your writing?
Does your story describe something that happened to you?			
Do you describe what happens in order?			
Do you use action words to describe what happens?			
Do you describe what you see, hear, smell, taste, and feel?			
Have you corrected mistakes in spelling, grammar, and punctuation?			

Use the notes in your chart and your writing plan to revise your draft.

Writing Report Card

Read your revised draft again or ask someone else to read it. Have the person who reads your paper complete the following Report Card. Revise your paper until you have no less than a Very Good Score for each item.

Title of paper: _____

Purpose of paper: _____ *This is a descriptive story. It describes something that*

_____ *happened to me.*

Person who scores the paper: _____

Score	Writing Goals
	Does the story describe an experience?
	Are the things that happen in the story in order?
	Does the story describe what the writer sees, hears, tastes, smells, and feels?
	Does the story have action words?
	Are the story's grammar, spelling, and punctuation correct?

☺ Excellent Score   ☆ Very Good Score   + Good Score
✔ Acceptable Score   − Needs Improvement

UNIT 4: Opinion and Comparative Writing

HOW MUCH DO YOU KNOW?

Read the persuasive paragraph. Answer the questions that follow.

The best building material for a house is bricks. A brick house always stays cool in summer and warm in winter. Houses made of wood need to be painted. Bricks never need to be painted. People get wet during the rainy season in a house made of straw. A brick house will keep people dry. Most importantly, a wolf cannot blow down a house made of bricks.

1. Draw a line under the topic sentence.

2. List the three main reasons the writer gives.

   _____

   _____

   _____

   _____

3. Which reason does the writer think is most important?

   _____

   _____

Analyzing a Persuasive Paragraph

> **A PERSUASIVE PARAGRAPH**
> - tells the writer's feelings, or opinion
> - lists reasons
> - asks readers to agree with the writer

Read the persuasive paragraph. Answer the questions that follow.

You should get involved in sports after school. There are many reasons for this. Perhaps the most important one is that exercise is good for your health. Exercise not only helps build strong muscles, it also helps keep your body from storing too much fat. A person who takes part in sports will usually have a healthier heart and lungs than a person who does not. In addition to being good for your health, sports can help you in other ways. Taking part in sports is a good way for you to make friends.

1. Draw a line under the topic sentence.

2. Does the topic sentence tell the writer's opinion?

   _____

3. What are the three main reasons the writer gives?

   _____

   _____

   _____

4. Which reason does the writer think is most important?

   _____

Evaluating to Draw Conclusions

> To write a persuasive paragraph, good writers support their feelings with good reasons.

Read each set of statements and the reasons that support it. Draw a line under the three best reasons.

1. Nathan pays for the bus to school, and he also buys his own lunch. Nathan thinks his allowance should be raised.

   a. His friend Orville gets more than he does.

   b. Lunch prices at school went up.

   c. He has been doing extra chores.

   d. Bus fares went up.

   e. He wants to start playing video games after school.

2. Dora's family is moving into a home that has two bedrooms for the three children. Dora thinks she should be the one to get her own room.

   a. She stays up later and doesn't want to disturb the others.

   b. She is the oldest and has more homework to do.

   c. She needs the extra space because she doesn't like to hang up her clothes.

   d. She needs the extra space for slumber parties.

   e. The other two children are boys, and it makes more sense for them to share a room.

Giving Reasons

Good writers give good reasons to convince the reader.

Read each sentence. Write the reason that best supports it. Choose from the reasons in the box below.

1. You should do your homework before watching television.

   _____

2. You should save part of every allowance.

   _____

3. After you take your jacket off, hang it up.

   _____

4. You should try to be on time for appointments.

   _____

5. It is a good idea to be friendly to new students.

   _____

REASONS

It's not thoughtful to keep others waiting.

Clothes left lying around make the room messy.

You will have money for something big later.

Television takes time away from studies.

You might make a good friend this way.

Combining Sentences

- Good writers sometimes combine sentences to make their writing more interesting.

- Two short sentences might have the same subject. The writer writes the subject once and then combines the two predicates in the same sentence.

Combine the predicates in these sentences.
Write the new sentences.

1. Kathy was tired. Kathy wanted her lunch.

   _____

   _____

2. She turned smoothly in the water. She headed for the other end
   of the pool.

   _____

   _____

3. Kathy wanted to win. Kathy hoped to set records.

   _____

4. Kathy won many races. Kathy got many awards.

   _____

   _____

5. Kathy practiced as much as possible. Kathy competed with stronger
   swimmers.

   _____

   _____

Proofreading Persuasive Paragraphs

Proofread the persuasive paragraphs, paying special attention to words or letters that may be out of order. Use the Proofreading Marks to correct at least seven errors.

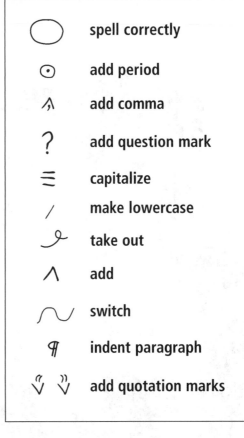

PROOFREADING MARKS

⬯	spell correctly
⊙	add period
⋏	add comma
?	add question mark
≡	capitalize
/	make lowercase
℘	take out
∧	add
∾	switch
¶	indent paragraph
⌄ ⌄	add quotation marks

Our class play coming is up next month, and everyone should hepl make it a success. It is true that not everyone can act in the play because there are not enough prats. Also, students some do not enjoy appearing on stage. Still, there is something for everyone do to. Those who do not wish to be on the stage can find plenty to do behind the scenes One such job making is scenery. Any student who likes to build can give time to this important job. We'll need staircases, walls, and street lamps for Act I. For Atc II we'll need scenery that looks like a beach

Another important job is making costumes. Students who enjoy different kinds of clothes will have fun this with job. We'll need soem special hats, some jewelry, and some old-fashioned beach clothes.

Write about Pets

Talk with a friend about different kinds of pets. Together, choose a pet you would both like to have. Draw a picture of that pet. Write a paragraph telling why that animal would be a good pet.

Write about Your Home Town

With a friend, make a list of things you like about your town. Then write three sentences that tell why your town is a great place to live.

Things we like about our town

_____   _____

_____   _____

_____   _____

_____   _____

Why Our Town Is a Great Place to Live

_____

_____

_____

_____

_____

Write Your Opinion

With a friend or two, consider this question: Should third-graders learn to do their own laundry? Write your answer and one reason that supports it. Everyone in the group shares answers. Then, using your reason and others from your group, write a persuasive paragraph to answer the question.

Should third-graders learn to do their own laundry?   ____ YES   ____ NO

Write about a Movie

With a friend or two, plan and write five sentences about a movie you all like. Revise and proofread your sentences.

_____

_____

_____

_____

_____

_____

_____

Draw a poster for your movie.

Write about Actions People Can Take

Here are statements about actions people can take. Check the statement that you feel the most strongly about and for which you have good reasons. Write a paragraph to convince someone to agree with you.

 Everyone should learn to cook.

☐ Everyone should go camping.

☐ Everyone should play a musical instrument.

_____

_____

_____

_____

_____

            _____

            _____

            _____

            _____

A Practice Alike-and-Different Paper

A BAT AND A BIRD

At night, a bat looks like a bird. Both bats and birds have wings and fly. They are also different in many ways. To understand how they are different, let's look at the Little Brown Bat and the American Robin.

The Little Brown Bat is about three inches long. It is about eight inches wide when its wings are open. The bat's body is covered with dark brown fur. Its ears are black.

The bat has hands with fingers and feet with toes. The wings are hands that have fingers covered with skin. At the ends of the fingers are strong claws. The bats use the claws to hang upside down from rocks. That's the way they like to sleep. They sleep all day. Then they come out when the sun goes down. That's when they fly to feeding grounds to eat.

The bats eat flies and other insects. They use a kind of radar to find their food. The bats let out quick, high sounds. We can't hear these sounds. The sounds bounce off the insects and return to the bats as echoes. Finding food this way is called "echolocation." Echoes let the bats find and catch their food.

Bats are mammals. This means that mother bats give birth to live babies. They also feed the babies milk from their bodies. A mother bat usually has only one baby a year. After it is born, the baby holds onto its mother. It drinks the mother's milk.

The American Robin is a bird, not a mammal. The male robin is colorful. Its beak is yellow. Its head is black, and its throat is white. The feathers on its breast are red like bricks. Most of its other feathers are grayish-brown.

The robin is about ten inches long. Its wings are covered with feathers. Like the bat, the robin has strong claws. It uses its claws to hang onto the

branches of trees while it sleeps. Bats sleep during the day, but robins sleep at night. They wake early in the morning to begin singing and searching for food.

Robins like to eat berries and insects. They also eat earthworms.

Like all birds, robins lay eggs. The mother may lay eggs two or three times each year. Each time, she may lay up to six bluish-green eggs. She lays the eggs in a nest made from twigs, roots, grass, and paper. The inside of the nest is lined with mud. Nests are built in trees and on building ledges.

When the eggs hatch, the parents feed their babies. The babies eat food their parents spit up. Robin parents feed the babies until they can leave the nest.

Bats and robins are alike in some ways. They have wings and claws, and they fly. Bats and robins are also different. They look different and eat different foods. They also have and care for their babies in different ways.

Look up in the early evening sky. Do you see something flying? Look closely, listen, and watch. Do you see a Little Brown Bat searching for food? Or is it an American Robin you see, settling on a branch for a night's rest?

Respond to the Practice Paper

Summarize the paper by making a chart. Use the chart below to list ways that Little Brown Bats and American Robins are alike and different.

AN ALIKE-AND-DIFFERENT CHART FOR LITTLE BROWN BATS AND AMERICAN ROBINS

How Little Brown Bats and American Robins Are Alike	How Little Brown Bats and American Robins Are Different

Analyze the Practice Paper

Read "A Bat and a Bird" again. As you read, think about how the writer wrote this paper. Write your answers to the following questions or directions.

1. When did the writer tell you what this paper was going to be about?

   _____

   _____

2. The writer tells you many things about Little Brown Bats. In order, list what the writer tells you. The first and last ones are done for you.

   - *what Little Brown Bats look like* _____

   - _____

   - _____

   - *how Little Brown Bats care for their babies* _____

3. The writer also tells you many things about American Robins. In order, list what the writer tells you. The first one is done for you.

   - *what American Robins look like* _____

   - _____

   - _____

   - _____

4. What does the writer do in the last two paragraphs?

   _____

   _____

   _____

Writing Assignment

Think about two animals you would like to write about. Think about how they are alike and how they are different. Use this writing plan to help you write a first draft on page 84.

Choose two animals you want to write about. Call them A and B.

A = _____   B = _____

With an adult's help, use books or the Internet to learn more about A and B. Learn about these main ideas: 1. how the animals look, 2. where the animals live, and 3. what the animals eat.

The main ideas are written outside each set of circles below. For each main idea, list what is true only about A in the A circle. List what is true only about B in the B circle. List what is true about both A and B where the two circles overlap.

MAIN IDEA:
How they look

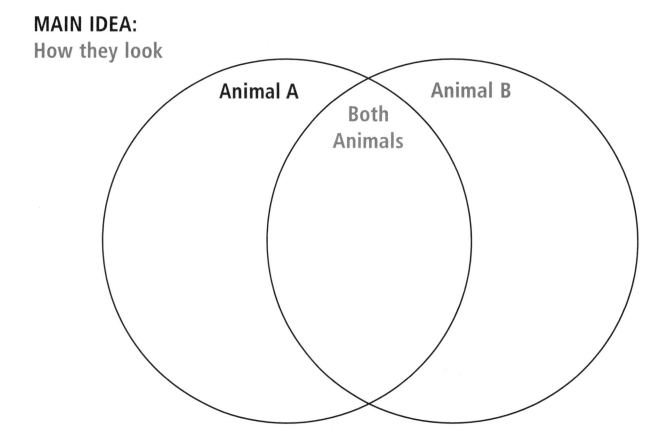

MAIN IDEA:
Where they live

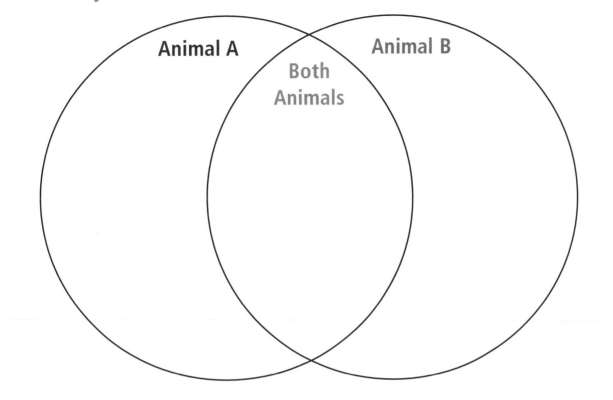

Animal A

Both
Animals

Animal B

MAIN IDEA:
What they eat

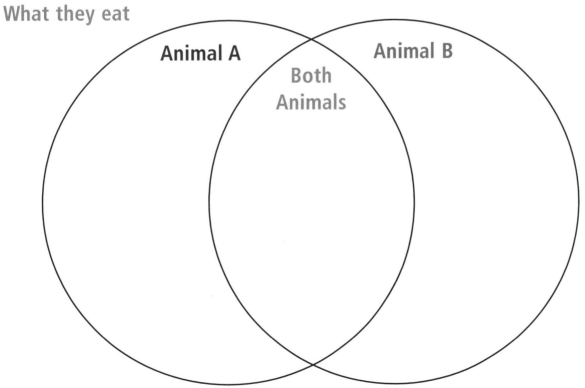

Animal A

Both
Animals

Animal B

First Draft

TIPS FOR WRITING AN ALIKE-AND-DIFFERENT PAPER:

- Find information about your animals.
- Organize the information you find into main ideas.
- Explain how the animals are alike.
- Explain how the animals are different.
- Use your last paragraph to summarize your main ideas in a new way.

Use your writing plan as a guide for writing your first draft of an alike-and-different paper. Include a catchy title.

_____

(Continue on your own paper.)

Revise the Draft

Use the chart below to help you revise your draft. Check YES or NO to answer each question in the chart. If you answer NO, make notes to remind yourself how you can revise, or change, your writing to improve it.

Question	YES ✔	NO ✔	If the answer is NO, what will you do to improve your writing?
Do you introduce the animals you will write about in your first paragraph?			
Do you tell how two animals are alike?			
Do you tell how two animals are different?			
Do you have more than one main idea?			
Do you organize the main ideas into paragraphs?			
Do you use details to explain each main idea?			
Have you corrected mistakes in spelling, grammar, and punctuation?			

Use the notes in your chart and your writing plan to revise your draft.

Writing Report Card

Read your revised draft again or ask someone else to read it. Have the person who reads your paper complete the following Report Card. Revise your paper until you have no less than a Very Good Score for each item.

Title of paper: _____

Purpose of paper: *This paper tells how two animals are alike and different.*

Person who scores the paper: _____

Score	Writing Goals
	Does the first paragraph tell what the paper will be about?
	Does the paper tell how two animals are alike?
	Does the paper tell how two animals are different?
	Is there more than one main idea?
	Are the main ideas organized into paragraphs?
	Does the last paragraph summarize what the paper is about?
	Are the paper's grammar, spelling, and punctuation correct?

☺ Excellent Score   ☆ Very Good Score   + Good Score
✔ Acceptable Score   − Needs Improvement

UNIT 5: Story

HOW MUCH DO YOU KNOW?

Read the story. Write or underline the answers to the questions that follow.

Pet Day at School

Yesterday we brought our pets to school. They made a lot of noise.

Mr. McGrath said, "Quiet down, dogs! Lie down, cats!"

We tried to help Mr. McGrath. My big dog got excited. She barked and barked. One cat scratched Jose's little dog. Even the ferret was making noise! Jenny didn't have any trouble with her pets. She had three big goldfish.

"You have wonderful pets, Jenny," Mr. McGrath said.

Finally, we all took our pets outside. Except Jenny, of course!

1. What is the setting for this story?

   _____

2. What is the problem Mr. McGrath must solve?

   _____

3. What kind of person is Mr. McGrath?
   a. unhappy
   b. silly
   c. a dog lover

4. Why didn't Jenny's pets cause problems?
   a. Jenny didn't bring any pets.
   b. Fish don't make noise.
   c. Jenny took them outside.

Analyzing a Story

A STORY HAS
- a title
- characters and a setting
- a problem that the characters must solve
- a beginning, a middle, and an ending

Read the story. Answer the questions that follow.

King Midas was a kind but silly man who lived in Greece long ago. One day, in exchange for a kindness, he was granted a wish. Without thinking, King Midas asked that everything he touched would turn to gold. The "golden touch," as it was called, made him very rich. Even his food and drink turned to gold. Midas could not eat or drink. The worst thing was what happened when his daughter ran to hug him. She, too, turned to gold. Finally, King Midas had to beg to have his golden touch taken away.

1. Who is the main character?

   _____

2. What is the setting?

   _____

3. What is the problem the character must solve?

   _____

4. Write one sentence that tells the middle.

   _____

5. Write one sentence that tells the ending.

   _____

Classifying Details as Real or Make-Believe

> To write a make-believe story, good writers use both real and make-believe details.

A. Read the paragraph. Then write three details that are real and three that are make-believe.

Alice sat by the stream with her sister. Just then a white rabbit ran by. The rabbit took a watch out of its vest pocket. It looked at the watch and declared, "I'm late!" Then the rabbit went down a hole in the ground.

Real

1. _____

2. _____

3. _____

Make-Believe

4. _____

5. _____

6. _____

B. Label each sentence *real* or *make-believe* on the line.

7. Alice walked in a garden. _____

8. She saw a caterpillar on a leaf. _____

9. The caterpillar asked, "Who are you?" _____

10. The Queen was a playing card. _____

Storytelling: Dialogue and Characters

Read the story with dialogue. Draw a line under the best answer to each question that follows.

"How do you feel?" asked the nurse, looking at the little boy in his hospital bed.

"My ear hurts," the boy answered sadly.

"Does it hurt a lot?" asked the nurse.

"Yes, but I can take it," answered the boy.

The nurse had known children like this before. The child, trying to be brave, would not say how much a pain hurts. The nurse had a special chart for children like this. It showed a ladder. The bottom rung of the ladder meant very little pain, and the top rung meant a lot. The nurse showed her chart to the boy.

"I'm on rung three," said the child, pointing to the middle of the ladder.

"Tell me when you're on rung four," said the nurse, smiling at him. "Then I'll give you some medicine for pain."

1. Who does the talking in this story?

   a. a nurse and a little boy

   b. a nurse

   c. a boy

2. What kind of person is the nurse?

   a. mean

   b. kind

   c. silly

3. What kind of person is the boy?

   a. active

   b. cruel

   c. brave

4. Who says, "I'm on rung three"?

   a. the doctor

   b. the nurse

   c. the boy

Avoiding Run-on Sentences

Good writers divide run-on sentences into
two or more sentences.

Revise each run-on sentence. Write two shorter
sentences to make the meaning clearer.

1. The baby opened the cabinet she took out
   all the pots.

   _____

   _____

2. The mother came into the kitchen she saw the mess.

   _____

   _____

3. The mother smiled at the baby she asked if it was fun.

   _____

   _____

4. The baby smiled back she was having a good time.

   _____

   _____

5. The mother sat on the floor she played with the baby.

   _____

   _____

Proofreading a Story

PROOFREADING HINT

To be a good proofreader, look for one type of error at a time. For example, proofread once for capitalization errors, once for punctuation errors, and once for spelling errors.

Proofread the stories, paying special attention to capital letters at the beginning of sentences. Use the Proofreading Marks to correct at least six errors.

PROOFREADING MARKS

◯	spell correctly
⊙	add period
⋀	add comma
?	add question mark
≡	capitalize
/	make lowercase
ℐ	take out
⋀	add
∿	switch
¶	indent paragraph
⌄ ⌄	add quotation marks

1.   Goldilocks sat down at the bears' table. the first chair she tried was too hard, and the second chair was too soft. the third chair felt just right. Next, Goldilocks tried all the oatmeal on the table The first bowl was too hot, and the second bowl was too cold. The third bowl tasted just right. after she had eaten the whole bowl of oatmeal, Goldilocks went upstairs for a nap.

2.   Fox looked up at the grapes on the vine. how delicious they looked! he decided to have some grapes four his lunch. The grapes were quite high, and it was hard for Fox to reach them. he stretched and jumped, but he couldn't get the grapes. Fox tried again and again. the grapes always seemed just out of reach. Finally, Fox gave up. he walked away, asking himself, "Who would want those sour old grapes?"

Write a Story

What might happen when a group of friends goes skating? With a friend or two, plan and write a story about a skating party.

Ideas for story

_____   _____

_____   _____

_____   _____

_____   _____

The Skating Party

_____

_____

_____

_____

_____

_____

_____

_____

_____

Write an Animal Story

Imagine that some mice and some geese become friends. Write three sentences telling what the animals will do. Draw a picture to go with your story.

_____

_____

_____

_____

_____

Write a Story for Younger Children

All kinds of animals make good stories. Here are some animals you may want to write about. Some are real. Some are make-believe. They may make great characters for your story. Add more animals to each list.

pony

raccoon

a frog that sings

a pet rhinoceros

Pick one of the animals from the list. Write a make-believe story about that animal to entertain younger children.

_____

_____

_____

_____

_____

_____

A Practice Story

THE MEETING OF THE MICE

Based on a Fable by Abstemius

Martha Mouse was very sad. Clever Cat had caught her brother. Martha wasn't the only sad mouse. Martin Mouse was also sad. Clever Cat had caught his mother and sister.

Martha talked to Martin. "I think," she said, "that we should have a meeting. Let's invite all the mice in town. If we work together, maybe we can find a way to be safe from Clever Cat."

Martin liked the idea. He said, "I think we should meet tonight. How about meeting in the basement of the school?"

Martha answered, "That's a good place. When shall we meet?"

"As soon as it is dark," said Martin. He looked to the left and to the right. "I wouldn't want to lose anyone on the way."

Martha agreed. "You're right. Until we have a plan, we can't be too careful."

Martha and Martin told every mouse they met to come to the meeting. They asked them to tell all their friends, too. That evening, as soon as the sun went down, the mice rushed to the school. Martha and Martin stood by the basement steps. They waved the mice forward. "Come in. It's safe, but hurry."

Hundreds of mice ran down the steps and into the basement.

Martha called the meeting to order. She stood before the other mice and said, "We have come together to discuss a big problem. Many of us have been hurt, and Clever Cat is the reason why. Some of us have lost our tails. Others have lost their fur. Even worse, he has eaten our friends and family."

The other mice squeaked in fright. Each one of them had a story. They wanted to tell how Clever Cat had hurt them, too. The stories took a long time. Finally, all the mice had spoken. Martha squeaked loudly to get everyone's attention. "It is clear. We have all been hurt. Now we have to find a way to keep Clever Cat away from us."

Many mice had ideas. Moby Mouse said, "Let's find a Dog to help us. Dogs chase cats."

Some mice liked the idea. But one said, "That won't help

unless the Dog is willing to chase Clever Cat all day and all night, too."

Another mouse stood up. "My name is Messy," he said. "I think we should hire a Mouse Guard to stand at our holes."

One of Messy's friends stood up to answer. "That won't work," he said. "We have so many holes. We would need too many Mouse Guards."

"That's true," said another mouse. "And besides that, we all have to go out of our holes every day to look for food."

Just then a young mouse stood up. "My name is Tom. I think I have a good idea. Let's hang a bell around Clever Cat's neck. Then we could hear Clever Cat coming. We would have time to run away."

All the mice clapped loudly. They squeaked for joy. They all agreed. This was a wonderful plan.

Just then, an old, old mouse stood up. He had been listening carefully all evening. He introduced himself. Then he said, "The bell is a very good way to keep Clever Cat away. It is a wonderful idea. It would work. But I have one question. Who will hang the bell around Clever Cat's neck?"

The mice were suddenly quiet. They looked at each other. Each mouse asked the next mouse, "Will you hang the bell around Clever Cat's neck?" Not one mouse said yes.

Respond to the Practice Paper

Write your answers to the following questions or directions.

1. A fable is a story that teaches a lesson. What is the lesson of this story?

   _____

   _____

   _____

2. The animals in fables often act like humans. How are the animals in this story like humans?

   _____

   _____

   _____

3. How would you describe the setting for this story?

   _____

   _____

   _____

4. Write a paragraph to summarize this story. Use these questions to help you write your summary:
   • What are the main ideas in the story?
   • How does the story end?
   • What lesson did this story teach?

   _____

   _____

   _____

   _____

Analyze the Practice Paper

Read "The Meeting of the Mice" again. As you read, think about how the writer wrote the story. Answer the following questions or directions.

1. Name ways the writer makes the characters seem human.

   _____

   _____

   _____

2. How does the writer make the story exciting?

   _____

   _____

   _____

3. Why does the writer use talking mice to tell the story?

   _____

   _____

   _____

4. Why is the last paragraph important?

   _____

   _____

   _____

   _____

   _____

   _____

Writing Assignment

Sometimes stories help us learn about ourselves. They help us think about what we can be or do. Think about writing a fable. Think about the answers to the questions in the boxes. Use your answers to help you write a first draft on the next page.

What is the lesson of the fable?

▼

Who are the animal characters?

▼

What problem will the characters have?

▼

How will the characters solve their problem? List what will happen in the story. Number each thing that happens.

First Draft

TIPS FOR WRITING A FABLE:

- Think about the lesson you want your fable to teach.
- Make your animal characters seem human.
- Plan a place and time for the story to happen.
- Give your characters a problem to solve.
- Write what happens in order.

Use your writing plan as a guide for writing your first draft of a fable. Include a catchy title.

_____

_____

_____

_____

_____

_____

_____

_____

_____

_____

_____

(Continue on your own paper.)

Revise the Draft

Use the chart below to help you revise your draft. Check YES or NO to answer each question in the chart. If you answer NO, make notes to remind yourself how you can revise, or change, your writing to improve it.

Question	YES ✔	NO ✔	If the answer is NO, what will you do to improve your writing?
Does your fable teach a lesson?			
Do your animal characters seem human?			
Do your characters have a problem?			
Do your characters solve their problem?			
Do you describe what happens in order?			
Have you corrected mistakes in spelling, grammar, and punctuation?			

Use the notes in your chart and your writing plan to revise your draft.

Writing Report Card

Read your revised draft again or ask someone else to read it. Have the person who reads your paper complete the following Report Card. Revise your paper until you have no less than a Very Good Score for each item.

Title of paper: _____

Purpose of paper: _*This is a fable. It teaches a lesson.*_____

Person who scores the paper: _____

Score	Writing Goals
	Does the story teach a lesson?
	Do the animals in this story seem human?
	Do the animals have a problem they must solve?
	Do things in the story happen in order?
	Do the animals solve their problem?
	Are the story's grammar, spelling, and punctuation correct?

☺ Excellent Score   ☆ Very Good Score   + Good Score
✔ Acceptable Score   − Needs Improvement

UNIT 6: Short Report

HOW MUCH DO YOU KNOW?

Read this short report. Underline the correct answer to each question.

Thomas Edison, Great Inventor

We see Thomas Edison's inventions everywhere. You often use his inventions. Without him, you could never turn on a light. Films are shown through one of his inventions. Music is listened to on one of his inventions.

Edison invented the electric lamp in 1879. He invented the movie projector and the phonograph. Edison is the greatest inventor who ever lived. He invented over 1,000 things!

1. The topic of this report is
   a. what Thomas Edison invented.
   b. how Thomas Edison invented the electric lamp.
   c. how a movie projector works.

2. What is one detail about the main idea?
   a. Thomas Edison lived in the 1800s.
   b. Edison invented the phonograph.
   c. You cannot turn on a light.

3. Which sentence states an opinion?
   a. Edison is the greatest inventor who ever lived.
   b. Edison invented the electric lamp in 1879.
   c. Films are shown through one of his inventions.

Analyzing a Short Report

A SHORT REPORT

- gives facts about one topic
- usually has more than one paragraph
- has a title that tells about the topic

Read this part of a short report.
Answer the questions.

A cold is caused by a virus. No one really knows how to prevent colds. Getting wet or chilled does not directly give you a cold. A chill, however, might put you in a weaker state than usual. Then, if a cold is going around, you will be more likely to get it.

Colds are usually caught by being near someone who already has one. The easiest way to catch a cold is from someone's sneeze. One person with a cold can give it to many other people in a crowd just by sneezing. If you have a cold, you should stay away from other people.

1. What is the topic of this report?

   _____

2. Write the sentence that states the main idea.

   _____

3. What is one detail about the main idea?

   _____

   _____

   _____

4. What might the topic of another paragraph in this short report be?

   _____

Classifying Fact and Opinion

To write a short report, good writers include
only facts about the topic.

Read each sentence. Write *fact* or *opinion* to tell what it is.

_____ 1. Liquid is a necessary ingredient of soup.

_____ 2. Chicken soup is better than turkey soup.

_____ 3. Gabriel's Restaurant serves lamb stew.

_____ 4. Gabriel's Restaurant serves good lamb stew.

_____ 5. The dishwasher is broken.

_____ 6. Every home should have a dishwasher.

_____ 7. We eat fish every Sunday.

_____ 8. Fish can be prepared in many ways.

_____ 9. Tuna is the most delicious fish you can buy.

_____ 10. The Japanese people eat a lot of fish.

_____ 11. Gabriel's Restaurant has one high chair.

_____ 12. People should not bring babies to restaurants.

Using Exact Words

Good writers use exact words to tell the facts about a topic.

Read each sentence. From the word list, choose a more exact word or phrase to replace each underlined word or phrase. Write a new sentence with the more exact words.

Word List

1. cat, dog, hamster ... bedroom, living room, kitchen
2. sleeping, napping, dozing ... an hour, about two hours
3. liver, hamburger, spinach ... chopped, grilled, steamed
4. run, walk, exercise
5. ball, stuffed mouse, exercise wheel

1. My <u>pet</u> sat on the sill of the window in the <u>room</u>.

   _____

2. He was <u>resting</u> for <u>a little while</u>.

   _____

3. Soon it would be time to eat some <u>food</u>, which I had <u>fixed</u> for him.

   _____

4. In the afternoon, my pet would want to <u>play</u>.

   _____

5. I need to buy a new <u>toy</u> for my pet.

   _____

Expanding Sentences

> Good writers make sentences clear by using
> adjectives and adverbs that describe the topic exactly.

Add an adjective or an adverb where you see this mark: *
The word or words you add should describe the thing or action.
Write your new sentences.

1. The * hummingbird built a * nest.

   _____

   _____

   _____

2. She found a * tree in a * place.

   _____

   _____

3. She wanted her nest to be * away from * cats.

   _____

   _____

4. She laid * eggs and sat on them *.

   _____

   _____

5. * the eggs hatched and the babies cried * for food.

   _____

   _____

Proofreading a Short Report

PROOFREADING MARKS

⬭	spell correctly
⊙	add period
⋀	add comma
?	add question mark
⣿	capitalize
/	make lowercase
℘	take out
⋀	add
∿	switch
¶	indent paragraph
⋁ ⋁	add quotation marks

Proofread the beginning of a short report, paying special attention to spelling. Use the Proofreading Marks to correct at least six errors.

The Passenger Pigeon

At one time there was a kind of bird called the passenger pigeon. The passenger pigeon was one of the most common birds in the wirld. In fact, their were once so many passenger pigeons that they darkened the skies. One sumar day these birds completely blocked the sunshine in New york. In 1808 poepel saw a flock of passenger pigeons one mile wide and 240 miles long! the flock had more than two billyon birds. The birds in that flock ate about 434,000 bushels of nuts, rice, and berrys every day.

No one now can see even won living passenger pigeon The last wild passenger pigeon was killed in 1906 in connecticut. In 1914 the last passenger pigeon in a zoo died. the passenger pigeon is extinct.

Write about Animal Nests

Many different kinds of animals build nests. With a friend or two, read about one kind of nest. Draw a picture of this nest. Together, write at least four sentences about the animal and its nest.

_____

_____

_____

_____

_____

_____

_____

_____

Make a Bird Book

Work with a friend or two. Together, read about one unusual kind of bird. Draw pictures to show what the bird looks like, where it lives, what it eats, and what is unique about it. Write two sentences to go with each picture.

WHAT IT LOOKS LIKE

_____

_____

_____

WHERE IT LIVES

_____

_____

_____

WHAT IT EATS

_____

_____

_____

WHAT IS UNIQUE ABOUT IT

_____

_____

_____

Write about Robots

With a friend or two, read about robots. Find out what kinds of jobs robots can do. Draw a picture of one type of robot, and write at least five sentences telling what that robot can do.

_____

_____

_____

_____

_____

_____

_____

_____

Write about Birds

With a friend, choose one kind of sea bird to write about. Together, find five facts about this bird. Then write five sentences about it.

SEA BIRD FACTS

_____   _____

_____   _____

_____

_____

_____

_____

_____

_____

_____

THE PONY EXPRESS

Long ago, there were no telephones or radios. There were no televisions or computers. There were no airplanes or cars. It was hard to get news all the way to California.

People who lived in California needed a quick way to get mail and news from the East. People wanted news about their friends and families. They also wanted to know what was happening in other places in the country.

Three people started a company called the Pony Express. The Pony Express carried mail and news throughout the West. On April 3, 1860, one Pony Express rider rode west from St. Joseph, Missouri. St. Joseph was the last stop for trains coming from the East. On the same day, another rider rode east from Sacramento, California. Both young men carried four bags of mail. The Pony Express was a lot faster than the stagecoach. A stagecoach took one month to deliver mail. A Pony Express rider could do it in ten days.

The Pony Express hired young men. They were often younger than 18 years old. They were skinny, too. No rider could weigh more than 120 pounds. That helped their ponies run longer and faster.

The Pony Express ponies were mustangs. These were small, wild horses. The horses were less than five feet tall. They galloped almost twelve miles an hour. The horses were smart. They learned their routes fast.

Besides riders, other people helped run the Pony Express. Some people worked at stations. One of their jobs was to take care of the company's horses. Riders picked up fresh horses when they stopped at stations.

The riders and the people who worked at the stations faced many dangers. One was the weather. Snowstorms slowed riders crossing the high mountains. Sandstorms slowed riders crossing the long, dry deserts. Wild animals like wolves were another danger. The riders also had to protect themselves from bandits. Bandits tried to steal the horses. They also took whatever money the riders were carrying.

Still, there were young men willing to ride for the Pony Express. Together, they covered 2,000 miles of land. A rider would leave one station and gallop to another. At his first stop, he slipped the mail cover off the saddle. He threw it on the saddle of a new horse. Then he was off again. This took about two minutes. Each rider rode 60 to 80 miles. He stopped every 15 to 25 miles to get a fresh horse. At the end of his trip, a fresh rider on a fresh horse took his place. The first rider stayed at his last station until it was time for his next job.

The Pony Express was successful. It delivered the mail faster than stagecoaches. But it only lasted about one and one-half years. It stopped running when telegraph wires reached California. By October 1861, the Pony Express closed its doors. Its riders and horses were no longer needed.

Respond to the Practice Paper

Write your answers to the following questions or directions.

1. What was the Pony Express?

   _____

   _____

2. Why did the Pony Express start?

   _____

   _____

3. What dangers did Pony Express riders face?

   _____

   _____

4. Write a paragraph to summarize information about the Pony Express.
   Use these questions to help you write your summary:
   • What is the report about?
   • What are some of the main ideas in the report?
   • What are some of the details in the report?

   _____

   _____

   _____

   _____

   _____

   _____

   _____

Analyze the Practice Paper

Read "The Pony Express" again. As you read, think about the main ideas the writer tells about. Write your answers to the following questions or directions.

1. When did the writer tell you what this paper was going to be about?

   _____

   _____

2. List the main ideas the writer tells about in order. The first and last ones are done for you.

   • *People in California wanted mail and news.* _____

   • _____

   • _____

   • _____

   • _____

   • _____

   • _____

   • *The Pony Express ended when telegraph wires reached California.*

3. The writer uses some special words like *mustangs* and *stations*. How does the writer make it easier for the reader to understand these words?

   _____

   _____

4. Why is the last paragraph important? What makes it different from the other paragraphs?

   _____

   _____

Writing Assignment

In a short report, writers write about one topic. They find information about the topic. Then they use the information to choose the main ideas for their report. They also choose details to help explain each main idea.

Think about writing a short report about something in the story you read. You might want to write about a famous Pony Express rider or mustangs. Use this writing plan to help you write a first draft on the next page.

The topic of this paper is:

_____

Main Idea of Paragraph 1: _____

Detail: _____

Detail: _____

Detail: _____

Main Idea of Paragraph 2: _____

Detail: _____

Detail: _____

Detail: _____

Main Idea of Paragraph 3: _____

Detail: _____

Detail: _____

Detail: _____

First Draft

TIPS FOR WRITING A SHORT REPORT:

- Find information.
- Take notes about important main ideas.
- Take notes about important details.
- Organize the main ideas and the details into paragraphs.
- Use the last paragraph to summarize your report.

Use your writing plan as a guide for writing your first draft of a short report. Include a catchy title.

_____

_____

_____

_____

_____

_____

_____

_____

_____

_____

(Continue on your own paper.)

Revise the Draft

Use the chart below to help you revise your draft. Check YES or NO to answer each question in the chart. If you answer NO, make notes to remind yourself how you can revise, or change, your writing to improve it.

Question	YES ✔	NO ✔	If the answer is NO, what will you do to improve your writing?
Do you write about one topic, or subject, in your report?			
Do you have more than one main idea?			
Do you organize your main ideas into paragraphs?			
Do you include details to help explain your main ideas?			
Do you "stick" to the topic?			
Do you use your last paragraph to summarize your report?			
Have you corrected mistakes in spelling, grammar, and punctuation?			

Use the notes in your chart and your writing plan to revise your draft.

Writing Report Card

Read your revised draft again or ask someone else to read it. Have the person who reads your paper complete the following Report Card. Revise your paper until you have no less than a Very Good Score for each item.

Title of paper: _____

Purpose of paper: _____*This is a short report.*_____

Person who scores the paper: _____

Score	Writing Goals
	Is this paper an example of a short report?
	Does the writer talk about one topic, or subject?
	Are main ideas organized into paragraphs?
	Are there details to explain each main idea?
	Does the report "stick" to the topic?
	Does the last paragraph summarize what the paper is about?
	Are the report's grammar, spelling, and punctuation correct?

☺ Excellent Score ☆ Very Good Score + Good Score
✔ Acceptable Score − Needs Improvement

Answer Key

Answers to the practice paper exercises questions may vary, but examples are provided here to give you an idea of how your child may respond.

Unit 1: Personal Narrative

p. 6
1. middle 2. beginning 3. ending
4. Responses will vary. Be sure reason given is valid.

p. 7
1. a. ending b. beginning c. middle
2. a. ending b. middle c. beginning

p. 8–9
1. 2, 3, 1
2. 1, 3, 2

p. 10
Responses will vary. Be sure reasons given are valid.

p. 11
1. receive 2. fortunate 3. bad
4. require 5. buy 6. least 7. cruel

p. 12–13
Uncle John has always been my favorite uncle⊙ What a surprise we all had last summer⊙ Late one evening there was a knock at the back door. Can you guess who was standing on our back steps❓ Of course, it was Uncle John⊙ He had a backpack, a small suitcase, and an armload of gifts.

Uncle John's present for me was a bright (blew)ᵇˡᵘᵉ T-shirt. it has a picture of an old castle on the back. Uncle John bought the shirt for me when he was traveling in England last year⊙ I wore that shirt every day (wile)ʷʰⁱˡᵉ Uncle John was staying with us⊙

Uncle John has been to many different parts of the world, and he loved telling us about his adventures. Listening to his stories was almost as much fun as going along on Uncle John's trips⊙

p. 20
1. The writer wrote "Save Jack" to explain how he became friends with Danny. Danny created a club to help Jack make friends at a new school. (Help your child clearly identify the purpose for writing. Guide him or her in supporting the answers with details from the story.)
2. First, Jack says he feels sad about leaving his friends. Later, Jack says he feels lonely, scared, and unhappy.
3. Jack seems happy and grateful to Danny for his help in making friends. For instance, in the last paragraph, Jack says, "Danny rescued me." (Look for a clear understanding of how Jack's feelings changed over time in the answers. Be sure your child includes details from the narrative to support his or her understanding.)
4. Be sure your child correctly summarizes the significant events of the story, paraphrasing as needed. Summaries should be organized in a thoughtful way, with the main ideas and important details clearly presented. Spelling, punctuation, capitalization, and grammar should be correct.

p. 21
1. Jack uses words like *I, me,* and *my* to show that he is writing about his own personal experiences.
2. Jack is the new kid at school, and he feels lonely and scared.
3. Danny, a boy at Jack's new school, actually solves Jack's problem. Danny starts the Save Jack Club. After a few days, the club includes everyone in Jack's class. The club is a way for Danny to get everybody to play soccer together.
4. In the first paragraph, Jack tells that this story is about being new in town and not knowing that Danny would become his best friend. In the last paragraph, Jack says he's more than just a new kid now. He also explains how Danny rescued him and became Jack's best friend.

Unit 2: Informative Writing
p. 26–27
Main idea: Animal tracks can tell you many things. 1., 2. Sentences will vary. Be sure that details refer to the main idea.
3. Paragraph B is more interesting because there are more details and examples.
4. Responses will vary, but should correctly give a detail from the paragraph.

p. 28
1. Main idea: The squid and the octopus look very different. a., b. Sentences will vary. Be sure that details refer to the main idea. 2. The squid and the octopus behave very differently. a., b. Sentences will vary. Be sure that details refer to the main idea.

p. 29
1. a. detail b. detail c. main idea
d. detail 2. a. detail b. detail c. detail
d. main idea

p. 30
Possible responses:
1. Paragraph B is more interesting because there are more details and examples.
2. Responses will vary but should correctly give a detail from the paragraph.
3. Responses will vary but should correctly give a detail from the paragraph.

p. 31
A sighted person can only imagine what it is like to be blind. Put a scarf over your eyes to block out light. Try to figure out what different foods are. Pretend to pay for something with coins. Try to walk into another room and sit at a table. Blind people can do all these things and more.

p. 32–33
Pond snails are useful in fish tanks. Ponds snails will∧ᵉᵃᵗ any extra food your fish leave. They will also eat some∧ᵒᶠ the moss that appears on the plant. The snails will eat some of the moss on the glass walls of the tank, too⊙ If you have (sevrel)ˢᵉᵛᵉʳᵃˡ pond snails in∧ᵗʰᵉ fish tank, you will not have to clean the tank as often.

If your pond snails are having babies, be sure to remove the snails∧ᶠʳᵒᵐ the tank. Fish will eat snail eggs. In the same way, if your fish are having babies, be sure ᵗᵒ∧ remove the snails. Snails will eat fish eggs.

There are many different kinds ᵒᶠ∧snails. Their different kinds ᵒᶠ∧ shells can add (grately)ᵍʳᵉᵃᵗˡʸ to the beauty of your fish tank. Not only are snails useful in keeping a tank clean, they also add interest to the tank.

p. 39
1. This how-to paper teaches how to make a drum and drumsticks.
2. The materials needed to make a drum and drumsticks include a round oatmeal box with a lid; two new, unsharpened pencils; foil; tempera paint and paintbrush; colored construction paper; glitter or other shiny things; glue; cord; an apron or old shirt; and old newspapers.
3. The most important thing is a round cardboard box with a lid.
4. The cord lets you hang the drum around your neck while you play it. (Help your child recognize this answer as an important detail. Discuss the importance of including details such as this in a how-to paper.)
5. Answers will vary, but look for indications of understanding, such as a clear description of the drum and drumsticks and a corresponding illustration. Spelling, punctuation, capitalization, and grammar should be correct.

p. 40
1. The writer states the purpose of the paper clearly, lists materials, gives clear,

step-by-step instructions, and gives helpful hints and details.
2. The writer tells what materials to collect and then says to make the drumsticks.
3. The writer lists the materials so they can be collected before starting the project. This saves time and makes the project easier to do.
4. Sequence words help the reader to understand the order of the steps.
5. Pictures and answers may vary. Check pictures to determine if your child understood the instructions.

Unit 3: Descriptive Writing
p. 45
1. a. 2. c 3. Casey has a tail. Casey said, "Meow."

p. 46
1. thick, red 2. round 3. green, orange
4. two-story, tiny 5. huge 6. little, brown
7. colorful 8. loud, banging 9. terrific
10. delicious 11. sweet, moist

p. 47
1. b 2. c 3. a 4. b

p. 48
1. look 2. feel 3. sound 4. look 5. sound
6. look 7. look 8. taste 9. feel 10. smell

p. 49
1. Guppies and goldfish are pets for fish tanks. 2. Catfish and snails clean harmful moss from the tank. 3. Black mollies and goldfish are lovely fish. 4. Guppies and black mollies have live babies. 5. Zebra fish and angelfish lay eggs.

p. 50–51

Have you ever heard of a person who likes washing dishes? My friend Dan really enjoy^s it. In fact, Dan washes dishes whenever he can. Dan pull^s a chair over to the sink so he can reach everything easily. Dan likes the lemony smell of the liquid detergent⊙ He squeezes the bottle gently and watches the liquid soap stream into the water. The soap mix^es with the hot water. Together, they create a mass of frothy white bubbles. When the bubbles almost reach the top of the sink, Dan turns the water off, then he carefully puts the glasses in the water.

Most of all, Dan like^s using a brand-new dishcloth. The cloth feel^s soft in Dan's hands. It has a clean smell, too. Dan rub^s each glass carefully with the soft, new cloth. Then he rinses the glass and sets it on the drainer.

p. 60
1. Matt is the pitcher for the White Caps.
2. The father tells Jess that he is being fair.

"I clap for people who do a good job," he says.
3. In the last paragraph, Jess says, "What a game!" Jess also says that next year, maybe she can be a White Cap.
4. Be sure your child correctly summarizes the significant events of the story, paraphrasing as needed. Main ideas should be organized logically and important details presented clearly. Spelling, punctuation, capitalization, and grammar should be correct.

p. 61
1. The writer uses descriptive action words and comparisons. The bat "whooshed" through the air. The runner "ran faster than a squirrel." The crowd's clapping "sounded like thunder," and the players "ran like swift cats." The ball looked "like a small, white bird."
2. Some of the words the writer uses are "kicked," "tagged," "smacked," and "popped."
3. The writer describes the feelings, sights, and sounds of the game. The writer uses descriptions, such as "The grass made my skin itch," "Their clapping sounded like thunder," and "The air was filled with claps, yells, and moans."
4. The players ran like the wind. The players swept past like locomotives.

Unit 4: Opinion and Comparative Writing
p. 66
1. The best building material for a house is bricks. 2. Possible responses:
A brick house stays cool in summer and warm in winter. A brick house will keep people dry. A wolf can not blow down a house made of bricks. 3. That a wolf cannot blow down a house made of bricks.

p. 67
1. You should get involved in sports after school. 2. yes 3. Possible responses:
Exercise is important for good physical health. Exercise builds strong muscles; exercise keeps the body from storing fat; and exercise builds a healthy heart and lungs. 4. It is important for your health.

p. 68
1. b, c, d 2. a, b, e

p. 69
1. Television takes time away from studies.
2. You will have money for something big later. 3. Clothes left lying around make the room messy. 4. It's not thoughtful to keep others waiting. 5. You might make a good friend this way.

p. 70
1. Kathy was tired and wanted her lunch.
2. She turned smoothly in the water and headed for the other end of the pool.
3. Kathy wanted to win and hoped to set records. 4. Kathy won many races and got many awards. 5. Kathy practiced as much as possible and competed with stronger swimmers.

p. 71–72

Our class play ~~coming is~~ up next

month, and everyone should ~~hepl~~ *help* make it a success. It is true that not everyone can act in the play because there are not enough ~~prats~~ *parts*. Also, ~~students some~~ do not enjoy appearing on stage. Still, there is something for everyone ~~do to~~ Those who do not wish to be on the stage can find plenty to do behind the scenes⊙ One such job ~~making is~~ scenery. Any student who likes to build can give time to this important job. We'll need staircases, walls, and street lamps for Act I. For ~~Atc~~ *Act* II we'll need scenery that looks like a beach⊙

Another important job is making costumes. Students who enjoy different kinds of clothes will have fun with this job. We'll need ~~soem~~ *some* special hats, some jewelry, and some old-fashioned beach clothes.

p. 80
Guide your child in organizing the information in a clear manner.
How Little Brown Bats and American Robins Are Alike: Both fly.; Both have wings.; Both have claws.; Both eat insects.
How Little Brown Bats and American Robins Are Different: The bat is 3 inches long, but the robin is 10 inches long.; The bat has brown fur and black ears. The robin has a yellow beak and feathers that are black, red, and grayish-brown.; The bat has wings made from clawed fingers covered with skin. It uses its claws to hang upside down. The robin has claws it uses to perch in trees.; The bat sleeps all day. The robin is active during the day and sleeps at night.; The bat uses a kind of radar called echolocation to find insects and flies.; The bat is a mammal, gives birth to one live baby at a time, and the baby drinks milk. The robin is a bird, lays 6 bluish-green eggs, and feeds its babies food that the parent spits up.; The robin builds a mud-lined nest out of twigs, roots, grass, and paper in trees or on a ledge.

p. 81
1. The writer tells that the paper is about how bats and birds are alike and different in the first paragraph.
2. What Little Brown Bats look like, What Little Brown Bats eat and how they find their food, What Little Brown Bats are, How Little Brown Bats care for their babies
3. What American Robins look like, When American Robins are awake and asleep, What American Robins like to eat, How American Robins build their nests, and How American Robins care for their babies
4. In the last two paragraphs, the writer tells the reader to notice how birds and bats are alike and different. This is a way for the

Answer Key 127

writer to restate the paper's main ideas and tie the first and last paragraphs together.

Unit 5: Story

p. 87
Possible responses:
1. school 2. Mr. McGrath finds the pets too noisy. 3. a 4. b

p. 88
Possible responses:
1. King Midas 2. Greece long ago
3. The golden touch has made his food, drink, and daughter turn to gold.
4. Even his food and drink turned to gold.
5. King Midas had to beg to have his golden touch taken away.

p. 89
1. Girl sits by a stream. 2. Rabbit runs by.
3. Rabbit goes down a hole. 4. Rabbit has a vest on. 5. Rabbit has a watch. 6. Rabbit talks. 7. real 8. real 9. make-believe
10. make-believe

p. 90–91
1. a 2. b 3. c 4. c

p. 92
1. The baby opened the cabinet. She took out all the pots. 2. The mother came into the kitchen. She saw the mess. 3. The mother smiled at the baby. She asked if it was fun. 4. The baby smiled back. She was having a good time. 5. The mother sat on the floor. She played with the baby.

p. 93–94
1. Goldilocks sat down at the bears' table. the first chair she tried was too hard, and the second chair was too soft. the third chair felt just right. Next, Goldilocks tried all the oatmeal on the table○ The first bowl was too hot, and the second bowl was too cold. The third bowl tasted just right. after she had eaten the whole bowl of oatmeal, Goldilocks went upstairs for a nap.

2. Fox looked up at the grapes on the vine. how delicious they looked! he decided to have some grapes ⓕⓞⓤⓡ his lunch. The grapes were quite high, and it was hard for Fox to reach them. he stretched and jumped, but he couldn't get the grapes. Fox tried again and again. the grapes always seemed just out of reach. Finally, Fox gave up. he walked away, asking himself, "Who would want those sour old grapes?"

p. 101
1. This story teaches that it takes more than just talk to get something done. All the mice had ideas for taking care of their cat problem, but no one had the courage to put the bell on Clever Cat. (Help your child

clearly identify the purpose of this story. Guide him or her in supporting the answers with details from the story.)
2. The mice act just like people do. They have different personalities and names. They have many different feelings. For example, the first sentence says that Martha Mouse was very sad. The mice have conversations, and they tell stories. (Look for your child's clear understanding of how the writer gives human traits to the animals in the story.)
3. The story takes place in the dark basement of a school. (Look for your child's understanding of setting. Help your child understand why the mice chose the basement.)
4. Be sure your child correctly summarizes the significant events of the story, paraphrasing as needed. Summaries should be organized in a thoughtful way, with the main ideas and important details clearly presented. Spelling, punctuation, capitalization, and grammar should be correct.

p. 102
1. Abstemius makes the animals seem human by giving them individual personalities. Martha Mouse has a take-charge personality. Martin is helpful but cautious. Also, the writer gives the mice lively conversation and shows them having many feelings, such as sadness, fear, and joy.
2. The writer makes the story exciting by having the meeting take place at night. The reader feels that Clever Cat might find the mice at any moment and pounce.
3. The writer uses the mice to say something about people. The mice are small and full of bustling talk, but not one of them wants to take a risk. The writer is really saying that people can be full of ideas but slow to act.
4. In the last paragraph, the reader sees that despite the mice's experiences, strong feelings, and grand ideas, not one mouse is willing to put the bell on the cat.

Unit 6: Short Report

p. 107
1. a 2. b 3. a

p. 108
1. colds 2. A cold is caused by a virus.
3. Responses will vary. 4. Responses will vary.

p. 109
1. fact 2. opinion 3. fact 4. opinion
5. fact 6. opinion 7. fact 8. fact
9. opinion 10. fact 11. fact 12. opinion

p. 110
Responses will vary.

p. 111
Accept any reasonable responses.

p. 112–113
At one time there was a kind of bird called the passenger pigeon. The passenger

pigeon was one of the most common birds in the ⓦⓘⓡⓛⓓ *world*. In fact, ⓣⓗⓔⓘⓡ *there* were once so many passenger pigeons that they darkened the skies. One ⓢⓤⓜⓐⓡ *summer* day these birds completely blocked the sunshine in New york. In 1808 ⓟⓞⓔⓟⓔⓛ *people* saw a flock of passenger pigeons one mile wide and 240 miles long! the flock had over two ⓑⓘⓛⓛⓨⓞⓝ *billion* birds. The birds in that flock ate about 434,000 bushels of nuts, rice, and ⓑⓔⓡⓡⓨⓢ *berries* every day.

No one now can see even ⓦⓞⓝ *one* living passenger pigeon⊙ The last wild passenger pigeon was killed in 1906 in connecticut. In 1914 the last passenger pigeon in a zoo died. the passenger pigeon is extinct.

p. 120
1. The Pony Express was a service started in 1860 that carried mail and news throughout the West. (Help your child include all the pertinent information in his or her answers.)
2. People who lived in California needed a quick way to get mail and news from the East. A stagecoach took one month to deliver mail. A Pony Express rider could do it in ten days. (Check to see that your child included all significant details.)
3. Pony Express riders had to ride through dangerous weather, such as snowstorms and sandstorms. They also faced wild animals and bandits.
4. Be sure that your child identifies the report's main ideas and includes significant details. Spelling, punctuation, capitalization, and grammar should be correct.

p. 121
1. The writer tells the topic in the title of the report. The first two paragraphs give important information that explains why the Pony Express began. Then, the Pony Express is introduced in the third paragraph.
2. People in California wanted mail and news.; Three people started a company called the Pony Express.; The Pony Express hired young men.; Riders rode wild horses called mustangs.; Other people worked for the Pony Express.; Pony Express workers faced many dangers.; Riders covered 2,000 miles by riding in relays.; The Pony Express ended when telegraph wires reached California.
3. The writer uses examples of simpler words to define each word that the reader might not know.
4. The last paragraph summarizes how the Pony Express was successful and why it ended.